A Ten-Minute History of the World

Queen Guinevere's Rules

Democracy is Not Impossible

essays loosely related to human rights

Guy Ottewell

state 2015 Nov

ISBN 978-0-934546-65-2

Universal Workshop

Raynham, Massachusettes, and Lyme Regis, England

www.UniversalWorkshop.com

This was a short talk I had to give in order to open an area meeting of Amnesty International groups. I was supposed to give a ten-minute survey of the Human-Rights State of the World. That seemed a bit much, and I was worrying about it as I made my way there. I decided it would be better to leave all that to question-and-answer time or brains-trust time. (If somebody wanted to know the state of affairs in Togo, somebody else might know or I could look it up in the last Amnesty International Report.) Instead there tumbled out of me something less ambitious, or at any rate less authoritative:

A Ten-Minute History of the World. (From a Zoroastrian Perspective.)

In Amnesty we hear and read so many horrible things, we surely wonder sometimes: will there ever be an end? Is it getting worse or is it getting better? Could the story, the multitude of stories, have a happy ending? Does it make any sense to be either optimistic or pessimistic? We must all be driven to wonder about this, but we don't seem to talk about it: I don't remember hearing any Amnesty presentation or reading any Amnesty paper about it. That's fine, in a way: we concentrate on the present, on the practical details, on getting on with the job; and maybe it would depress us if we looked into it and had to realize that there will *not* be any happy ending. I, however, am an optimist—kind of. Perhaps that has to be typical of Amnesty members or we wouldn't keep on, but there are optimists and pessimists among us, and I used to imagine a debate we might have in our group, as a program at one of our meetings, between me and a friend who was a pessimist, who was cynical about all powerful people and institutions and who shook her head wisely at any suggestion that things might ultimately improve. For such a person to keep working in Amnesty is very creditable: it's the ultimate braveness to keep striving for a cause when you're convinced it's hopeless. If we had held such a debate—well, I never won an argument with that lady, and I'm sure this wouldn't have been the first. Now I can try holding the debate with myself, though I'm not sure I'll win even then . . .

What *is* the general trend of world history—upward or downward? When I was a little boy my passion was ancient history, and I wished I was living in the fourteenth century B.C. along with Ikhnaton and Joshua and Minos and Hercules . . . I soon learned the general scheme into which history was organized: the trend was upward, from the long slow Old Stone Age to the Neolithic (farming) and the Bronze Age (cities and civilization) and the Iron Age (empires). And so on up to Athens (mind), and the Renaissance (art), and the Enlightenment (reason), and the Industrial

Revolution (science). In fact I think the middle class in England was still essentially living in the Victorian age (in spite of its having come to a crashing end in the long compound event called World Wars One and Two); the main idea was Progress, a Victorian idea, always Progress, even though we tended rather unfairly to measure it *from* the Victorians: "How far we've come from Victorian ideas!" It was obvious that things were being discovered and invented and improved every day, and the pace, too, was ever quickening, onward and upward, new medicines, better schools, bright new solutions. Our minds too must be improving, or at least our collective mind, and there would be no problem we could not solve.

Unknown to me, the history books I read didn't include certain things. They didn't mention how the Assyrians impaled thousands of people. Innocent villagers, just because the Assyrian king wanted to add their lands to his conquests, impaled—that means, stakes through the groin and out of the throat—by the thousands. Massive cruelties happen in our world too, but think of the scale in the earlier times: then, it was tens of thousands out of perhaps fifty million, as against the world population now of five thousand million. There came the Persians who invented crucifixion, the Romans who added to it such details as short crosses so that the crowds could torture the naked crucified, and so on up to the English who invented hanging-drawing-and-quartering. For a witness to a Roman exhibition of wild oxen goring Christian maidens, it would have been impossible to be an optimist about humanity. The history books from which I got facts about king's reigns and battles didn't go into that sort of detail, didn't describe how the besieged Carthaginians in their desperation sent children "through the flames to Moloch" and how when the Romans finally took Carthage they galloped through the streets over the heads or the feet of people, depending on which way they were thrust down into the holes in the ground. No, it would be unwise to wish yourself back into an earlier century. It's even unwise to be too scathing about the shortcomings of our friends the police. In eighteenth-century England, just before police were invented, there was no idea that part of the business of government was to protect people: if you were caught by the robbers who operated openly in the streets or the highwaymen who infested the countryside or the armed gangs that besieged farmers in their houses and tortured them to make them tell where they kept their money, your only hope was to bargain for your life.

I'll pass around this picture in this book, which has nothing to do, in a way, with human rights—the book is called *The Making of the English Landscape*. Look at this scene from hell: a view of the coal-mining and iron-making district called the Black Country, in 1866. In the most catastrophic parts of Eastern European cities today you couldn't see anything quite like this; and then there was no environmental movement, there was no restraint.

There is an old saying that "You can't change human nature." But it has changed. One example pointed out in a book called *The Dictionary of Misinformation*, by Tom Burnam, is the aid sent by Castro's Cuba to its ideological enemy, Somoza's Nicaragua, devastated by an earthquake in 1972. Such an act would have been incomprehensible to even the best of the ancient Greeks, who if they heard that a catastrophe had overwhelmed some other land or even some other Greek city would have exulted in it as a just punishment sent from the gods. (Incidentally, Castro's earthquake-relief aid was embezzled by Somoza, causing the popular outrage that led to his fall. This only illustrates that the changing of human nature is piece-meal.) Today when a calamity in Ethiopia or Somalia has gone on too long we hear of "compassion fatigue"; but it is only a recent development for countries to show such compassion among themselves at all.

Not only can human nature change, but a lot of what we take for "human nature" is just the ways of our own society. When I went to be a student at Cambridge, I discovered I wasn't allowed to study my passion, archaeology, without anthropology: they were combined, so that reluctant-ly I had to take archaeology along with anthropology, a subject of which I had barely heard. This was a stroke of luck. I discovered that anthropolo-gy is the most important and beautiful subject there is: not excluding phi-losophy, or astronomy from which I now make a living, or theology, or English literature! I'm talking about social anthropology; there's also phys-ical anthropology, which means races and bones and blood-types, and is interesting too, but the subject of subjects is social anthropology. I'd rec-ommend to the students who are going to go on to college that you take social anthropology if you get a chance. It's the study of human life-ways. It is *the* mind-broadening subject. It will expand your mind more than L.S.D. ever pretended to. You find that the way we live is only one of many valid ways for human societies to live.

(I wish I could *require* candidates for national or international polit-ical office to have studied anthropology.)

More recently I got into reading anthropology books again, and realized something else besides the kaleidoscopic beauty of the variety of human cultures and their preciousness and the tragedy of the progressive disappearance of them before they can finish teaching us their secrets, much as the disappearing plants of the rainforest could be teaching us their medical and nutritional secrets. This is that there is a pattern, a trend, that is contrary to the old idea of the upward trend. The societies of the earliest and smallest kind, the bands of hunter-gatherers, which are still represented by the Bushmen and the Australian Aborigines (or those of them keeping to traditional ways), are the best. They are, in general, cooperative, egalitarian, non-sexist, with hardly any hierarchy or violence. The division of labor tends to be just that the men do the hunting and the women do the collecting of nuts and roots, which is more important because it produces more; food is shared, everybody regarding each other as kin; people work only if and when they feel like it, not much time being required, so that most of life is spent in leisure; population growth is slow, partly because breast-feeding goes on for a long time. Hunter-gather camps, according to one source, "stay relatively free of the vermin and disease that still plague settled societies."

When population pressure reaches the point that the pigs in the forest are hunted out and the society has to move to domestication—in other words, when you get the Neolithic revolution, and the hunter-gatherer band society passes into an agricultural, village society—it's been found that people have to work longer for less nutrition. There is more total production, but the share per person goes down; and it goes down more for some, because you also get the beginnings of organization and division of land and accumulation of goods, and hierarchy, and some persons bossing others and getting larger shares. And so on into the transition to cities, and stratified societies, with division of labor, money, kings and priests and scribes and tailors, lords and peasants, harems and beggars and territorial wars, exterminations and prisons and slavery. For the majority of people, work takes up all of every day, nutrition is less than ever, life is shorter, and none of it is your own. The bottom is reached in those societies which the old history books call glorious: the empires. The Assyrians, the Persians, the Romans, and over in the New World the Incas, who I think had the most stratified, monolithic, theocratic, rich, cruel, and utterly terrifying empire ever.

So what is the general trend? We have to be careful of trends: there really isn't any general trend but a composite of many trends, any of which can be upset and sent in different directions by an incident or even an individual. To give one celebrated example, the Battle of Salamis,[1] in which a few thousand people from a tiny democracy, debating and quarreling with each other, hardly able to agree on a common course of action and failing to get the cooperation of their equally fractious neighboring little cities, managed to pull themselves together and, because they really were interested in staying free, defeated—stopped themselves from being run over by—the hugest military empire the world had ever seen. That was rather as if

---

[*] Or Marathon, ten years earlier. The name has a more romantic ring, and the idea of Marathon as turning-point in history is the theme of a book called *Marathon, the Story of Civilizations on Collision Course*, by Alan Lloyd (1973). But the naval battle of Salamis was the real crisis, and Themistocles the individual; see the brilliant short description of the whole sequence in a classic book, *The Glory That Was Greece*, by J.C. Stobart (1911).

the people of, say, Hong Kong . . . Well, let's not pursue invidious contemporary analogies. Actually, this may be an exaggeration, there were reasons why the Athenians won the battle of Salamis, but it did hang in the balance and if it had gone the other way we wouldn't have had Aeschylus or Aristotle, perhaps we wouldn't have had rational thought or democracy, the trend might have been ever downward to a world empire, a 1984, a world of human ants.

I think the world trend is, at a first approximation, like this, hammock-like, down from the hunter-gatherer band societies to the empires, up again to our state of somewhat improved and improving knowledge and compassion, but this graph is over-simplified in two ways. First, of course, it should be different curves in different parts of the world, there are hunter-gatherer bands still clinging on and empires still forming. More important, the graph is a shallow image: there is a deeper dimension to it, and that is: potential. The band and village societies are a beautiful ideal, and I hope that we can still learn from them and rediscover some of their happiness—that is, use them as models for some of the aspects of better patterns of living we may get back to in the future. We might be able to get back to village life, extended families, cooperation instead of hierarchy, small units, low population, longer breast-feeding. But do we want to be without books, computers, string quartets, science, travel, hospitals? The so-called simple societies were very far from simple, but they were without potential—that's not what I mean—they were full of potential, but the potential lay centuries ahead, the potential for each individual in them was low. That's the deeper dimension to this one end of the hammock-shaped graph. The opposite for the other end. The potential at our end is very high. It is so high as to be very dangerous. It is now a high-speed race between trends.

Human nature has improved. We have spreading social awareness, the environmental movement, low-interest loans for women starting small enterprises in Africa, "compassion fatigue," the self-recovery of Eritrea, the War Crimes Tribunal, the International Crisis Group, the Carter Center, Amnesty International. We *are* on an upward trend. But threatening it are two other trends: the population explosion, and the explosion of technology. The population explosion simply has to stop. There is nothing good about it. It underlies the increase in human-rights violations as well as every kind of worsening social and environmental trend.

The technology-explosion has the potential for magnifying whatever other trend prevails. It gives Saddam Husein multiplied power to dive-bomb cities with poison gas and drain marshes to exterminate independent tribes and track and torture dissidents electrically and electronically, and gives multi-national corporations multiplied power to drive people out of rainforests and drive in logging-roads and mines and pipelines. On the other hand it multiplies information and reaction, journalism, television, faxes, the internet—human inter-consciousness.

The ancient Persians had a religion called Zoroastrianism, a dualistic religion. There was Ahura Mazda, "Lord of Light," and opposed to him there was the evil spirit, Ahriman. The difference from Jehovah and Satan was that Ahura Mazda and Ahriman were evenly matched. No one knew what the ultimate outcome would be. It depended on how many humans joined each side, and how hard they worked. You, as an individual, might tip the balance.

This may be a travesty; Zoroastrianism, which had offshoots called Mazdaism and Manichaeism and today survives in the Parsees of India, went through transformations and corruptions like all religions—certainly Darius, who made Zoroastrianism the state religion, but who personally put his defeated rival Phraortes to the most ghastly of all the ghastly deaths I have ever heard of, was not a good Zoroastrian in my sense—and my picture of it may be my own invention. I think it is a useful picture: the outcome does depend on us individuals. The trends are fighting, at an alarming speed: the ultimate shape of the graph can be influenced by our jumping onto one of them. Put another way, as Gandhi said (roughly), "What you do is very little, but it is very important that you do it." Or, another way: if you're not part of the solution, you're part of the problem. We in America, even those of us who lead what we consider a simplified life, consume on average forty times as much as people in India do, so we are part of the cause of their misery; we have a debt. If you do nothing but earn a living and have fun, you keep building up your debt; if you write one Amnesty letter a year, you certainly help toward tipping the balance; I haven't worked out where the break-even point is, how much you need to do to be shrinking your debt; perhaps we should leave it by saying that we don't all need to be striking blows for Ahura Mazda all the time, we just need to do a useful thing whenever the opportunities come by.

This was a talk for a meeting of a local humanist group, but the method proved useful in gatherings of other kinds.

Queen Guinevere's Rules

This is about what may seem to be a minor subject: a suggested way of sometimes conducting meetings, such as those of this group.

Most meetings that people hold go along under some sort of rules, even if they're unstated or chaotic. There are some highly formalized systems: for instance, the well known Robert's Rules of Order, which are defined in a largish book and are used in many parliamentary-type meetings, from governmental bodies to small societies. Of course their purpose is to ensure fairness. One disadvantage they have is that most people don't really know them, and therefore get confused and frustrated. And rules of this type are designed for certain types of meeting, where an object is to arrive at votes and carefully defined resolutions.

I want to tell you about another set of rules, which we sometimes use at our Amnesty International meetings, and which are very much simpler. In fact this particular system has only five rules. It might be called the Round-the-Circle system. When you hear that, you can guess most of it already.

For fun we could call it King Arthur's Rules. The legend is that when the knights sat down for supper, they quarreled as to who was more senior and should sit nearer the head of the table. So King Arthur had a Round Table made. (This table, or what is supposed to be it, is still hanging up in Winchester Cathedral; it looks like a huge dartboard.) He made the knights sit around this table, where there wasn't any head. There wasn't any *president* (a word which comes from Latin meaning "sitting foremost").

That still leaves a problem, because surely the ones sitting closer to the king could boast they were more important. So let's say we're describing the system on a night when King Arthur wasn't there—he was off on a campaign, or sick in bed upstairs. So the knights around the table really were all equal. We could call it Queen Guinevere's Rules. I suppose Queen Guinevere sat at the table too. You couldn't expect, in those times, that she'd rank as high as the King, but surely she ranked equal with the knights, besides being cooler-tempered. And they tended to enjoy the conversation more on such an evening.

Here are Queen Guinevere's five rules:

The first is that you should be sitting in some approximation to a circle. Maybe it can work in other settings: you could say "The order is going to be along the first row, and then along the second row, and so on, and then back to the beginning and start again." But the other four rules are definitely easier to apply when people are in a circle, rather than a classroom-like array. It makes a fundamental difference to communication when people can see each other's faces. (For this reason—and also for introducing a note of informality—I like a rough circle or oval or pentagon better than a rectangle.) People may or may not be around a table, or have a circle of tables in front of them; that depends on whether it's the type of meeting where people will want to take notes, deal with sheaves of paper, and circulate signup sheets.

The second rule, and the essential one, is that everyone has a chance to speak in turn, going strictly around the circle. The first person says what he or she wants to say. Then the next person to the right (or left); then the next . . . It's a good idea to go sometimes leftward, sometimes rightward.

People don't have to be answering or following on to each other in any way, though they usually do. They can say *what they like*. (This is a big difference from parliamentary rules, where you get ruled "out of order" if you are not, say, speaking in favor of the current amendment to an amendment.)

For instance the third person, whose name is perhaps Janet, can say: "That isn't true, Frank . . ." Or she can say: "I liked what you just said. Thank you." Or she might say: "I'm new here, I really don't have anything to say." Or she might say: "I think it's relevant to tell you a story about what happened to me on the way here . . ." Or she might say: "I have an announcement. Our next meeting will have to be canceled because . . ."

The third of Queen Guinevere's Rules is simply this: brevity. No one speaks for too long. What about that person who said "I want to tell a story . . ."? You have to have a rule that no one should take more than, say, three minutes. The real rule is that everyone is encouraged to keep it *as short as they can*; if they get up to three minutes it's a minor emergency, the moderator should intervene.

The keep-it-short rule is somewhat self-enforcing. As you'd find, participating in a meeting of this kind is *fun*. People hope after a while that they may get at least one more turn. There is some collective impatience with anyone who slows it down too much.

Yet the brevity rule should be, and tends to be, applied considerately. While a person is using his turn to speak, you should try *not* to show impatience. Don't start fidgeting to remind him to wrap it up. Why should you?—your turn is coming. It's very disconcerting, it cuts into the person's freedom to speak. It's always happening in non-round-the-circle meetings.

The fourth rule is rather a detail. Janet may use her turn to ask a question: "You, Frank" (on the other side of the circle), "what did you mean when you said . . ." or "Could I ask you something about how the plan you suggested would work?" When that happens, the person she's asked answers—also within the brevity rule. And then it goes back across and on as before, that is, not to Janet but to the next person on her right. There's no deviation from this: no back-and-forth between Janet and the person she asked the question of. And no one else can pipe up and say "I'd like to add to Frank's answer" or "Frank got that wrong . . ." If you want to correct the answer Frank gave, you can do so when it comes to your turn.

Or Janet's question may be a general one. "I'm new to this group," she may say, "and I want someone to explain to me what 'Co-Group' means" or "what the policy is on the death penalty." Then any old member—that is, any long-established member—can take it on himself to answer, briefly, perhaps adding that she can get more information by talking after the meeting, or by picking up a pamphlet. Again, nobody else should add—out of turn—to the person's answer. And again, the turn then goes back across and to the next person on Janet's right.

Nobody should ask a question *of* Janet during her turn or as she finishes it. That can quickly lead to a lengthened turn for her or to general breakdown of round-the-circle procedure. Keep your question till it's your turn.

The fifth rule is about what happens if someone uses their turn to introduce an important announcement or proposal, or an action for which a decision or volunteers are needed. There can then be a temporary suspension of round-the-circle rules. The person must be allowed to speak for as long as the matter demands (still not too long, we hope) and people from all around the circle must be allowed to ask questions or offer suggestions or their help. Then, as soon as this matter is dealt with, the round-the-circle rules can resume. The speaker may be allowed *also* to have her brief say about whatever else is on her mind; then the turn goes on to the next person on her right, as before.

Those, then, are the five simple rules. You are sitting in a circle. The turn to speak keeps going to the next person. Each person can say *anything*, but must be reasonably brief. Any question goes across the circle to whoever answers it, but then the turn goes strictly back to the next person whose turn it would have been. The rules are suspended—not ended—if someone brings up a matter requiring general questioning, volunteering, or decision-making.

Now some comments. First, about when the rules are used. I'm not saying that this round-the-circle system has to be the way a whole meeting is run. It could be just a segment of the meeting. The group could have the habit of always having at least one round-the-circle time, giving everyone a chance to relieve their feelings. That's what we do now at our Amnesty meetings. It could be the last thing in each meeting, or take the place of the "Any Other Business?" part of conventional meetings. I think it is the best way of handling "Any Other Business." When this comes on the agenda of a formal meeting, it still tends to be dominated by those who stick their hands up most aggressively, or who have spoken to the moderator in advance.

Or, the round-the-circle time could be a substitute for a "Program." That's how we first introduced it in Amnesty, at a meeting for which no speaker or video had been planned.

Or, the round-the-circle part of the meeting could be started ad hoc, when some situation arises that seems to call for it. I'll say a little more about this, under the rubric of "advantages."

A useful application is just before a vote. You can say "Wait: before we take a vote, let's go once around the circle." Sometimes, going around the circle and hearing each person's opinion, which is like an *explained* vote, makes actual voting unnecessary: it turns into an arrival at a consensus.

The round-the-circle system *can* be used for the whole meeting. We just did so, at our last meeting. The person who was to have been the moderator did not show up, so the one who had to get the meeting started did the usual preliminary things—mainly asking everybody to introduce themselves, *around the circle*—and then suggested that we go around the circle for the whole of the rest of the meeting; and it worked. No fewer than seven of those important pieces of business came up—four big impending events, one proposal of a new activity, and two actions needing letter-writers—and the rules were suspended for them, and then resumed. At a conventional meeting these, or those of them that had been foreseen, would have been placed on an agenda. But it did not seem to matter that they did not come up in logical order. I must admit that we got all around the circle only once.

Here are some advantages (and disadvantages) I see in using Queen Guinevere's Rules.

First, nearly everyone loves it. After the first time we did it in Amnesty as a program, some people said "Let's do this at least every second or third time" or even "every time!"

Second, and perhaps first in importance: the quiet people get their chance to say what's on their minds. They may not want to, they may say "Pass" the first time around, but they may get drawn in the second time. It's much easier to speak when your turn comes than to speak when some helpful high-profile person suddenly says "What do *you* think?"—whereupon you have the feeling of being picked out as a shy person. It isn't only shy people who get squeezed out of other kinds of meeting. A few, generally but not always men (I'm one of them), get to talk several times because their will to do so is more aggressive. Believe it or not, I've been in many meeting situations (usually in Amnesty conferences) where I wanted to say something but I trembled and probably blushed as I wondered whether to go for my chance—because it was a large meeting, chairperson-dominated, I'd have to stand up or go to some microphone, there might be a general or official impatience . . . Haven't you felt that? In a Queen Guinevere meeting, your turn is coming whether you want it or not. If you really don't want it, you can say "I pass."

It is very noticeable that the temperature and even the noise of a meeting drop as it moves into this procedure. People cease competing for their turns, shooting their hands up, itching for others to stop speaking.

I've often told myself (seldom remembered) to pause for a second before speaking. This is impossible if you're competing for a turn to speak: you lose it.

Queen Guinevere's Rules are democratic. I hardly need to say any more about this, it's so manifest. Maybe you can think of a way such a procedure could become undemocratic, but at the moment I can't.

Another advantage: sometimes it's good to have to stop and ponder for a while before retorting to what someone said. While Frank is speaking, reactions to what he's saying are boiling in your head, you're bursting for him to end, and then you cut in with your response which contains all the good points you wanted to make—or so you think. But two minutes later you're thinking, damn, I shouldn't have said this, I forgot to say that . . . If you have to wait for your turn around the circle, you're forced to have time to cool down a bit, and to get your thoughts in order; and when your turn comes your response is likely to be more complete and yet shorter, and probably more polite.

It may be an advantage or a disadvantage of round-the-circle rules that they tend to have you making notes. If Frank says something that you really want to respond to, but it isn't your turn until ten later, you may forget unless you jot yourself a note. An aesthetic disadvantage, if you like, is that a round-the-circle meeting is artificial: it's less like conversation, less like a play, less dramatic!

An objective disadvantage is that it may take too long, and this of course gets more serious the larger the number of people. The limit is perhaps reached at about thirty. People may want to go around twice, or three times, but it may become barely possible to go around once. At our Amnesty meetings, I personally would love to go around as long as we like, past midnight, but others have to leave, put children to bed . . .

(But a meeting where a few people dialogue or ramble may be just as long, and leave the rest dissatisfied.)

Another advantage of round-the-circle rules is that they're so simple you can switch to them with minimal explanation. Say the moderator decides for some reason that the moment has come to switch to them; or someone interjects: "Hey, I suggest we go to Queen Guinevere Rules now," and there are nods of agreement from those who know what is meant. The moderator can then very easily say: "That means, for those new to our meetings, that we go around the circle; each person has a *short* turn to say *whatever* they want." You don't need to mention rule number one, because you're already sitting in a circle; nor do you need to mention, at this point, rules four and five: those can be briefly described if and when someone does ask a question or raise a time-needing piece of business.

A final and very great advantage of the round-the-circle rules is that they defuse tense situations. Anyone can say "I think we need to handle this by going around the circle," and the moderator can give the brief explanation.

For instance, confrontation or potential nastiness may loom, as when two people start arguing across the meeting, threatening to distort it. There was a time when a religious fanatic spoke up at the founding meeting of a humanist society. He virtually took over for a while, not just by speaking but by having everyone want to answer him; he had the whole meeting becoming what it didn't want to be. Switching to round-the-circle rules solves this kind of situation. You wouldn't be suppressing the trouble-causer: he could say what he likes when his turn comes—within three minutes. But other people could, when their turn comes, say for instance: "I move we should *close off* that subject." That would be understood to mean close it off when there's been one complete around-the-circle; after the around-the-circle the moderator would say, "All right, closed off now," or take a vote on it. Or, less drastically, someone could say "Our friend can say what he likes when it's his turn, but I suggest we don't answer him any more; we're here to talk about Humanism." Or: "I don't think anything useful is going to come out of debating this matter here, but I'd be willing to talk one-on-one with our friend if he'll give me his telephone number." Or, "This may be important, but I suggest we drop it for now and consider scheduling a future program on it."

That's the end of my pitch for Queen Guinevere's Rules. I'd like to suggest, if we have time and if it meets with everyone's approval, that we try it here and now: go around, and all give your comments if any, constructive or destructive, on Queen Guinevere's Rules, and of course on anything else under the sun.

This is a somewhat shortened and friendlier version of a piece called "Democracy, Let Us Invent It" that I put in Issue 1 of my short-lived magazine In Defense of Variety. *I'm throwing it in here because the publishing system told me there was a minimum of 24 pages.*

Democracy is not impossible

There once was a political party in Turkey called Demokrat. It became very undemocratic, was overthrown in 1960 by a military coup and its leaders were executed. The succeeding Justice Party, to trick those who had formerly voted "Demokrat," adopted as its emblem an Iron-Gray Horse; in Turkish, Demir-kir at.

So those syllables sometimes don't mean very much. We believe we live in a system where they mean more: *demos* is "people" and *kratia* is "power." It was the invention of Greek city-states, in which the whole demos (other than women, children, and slaves) gathered in a public place to decide on laws or to ostracize over-prominent citizens. And more recently there was democracy in some of the town meetings of early New England, attended by property-owning men. But no existing nation is literally a democracy.

The several hundred million people of a modern country do not meet to argue out their legislation. They elect representatives, and these representatives decide the legislation. This is not really democracy; it is representative government. The Greeks, had they ever experienced such a system, might have called it allocracy—government by others.

Franz Jonas, elected president of Austria in 1965 after a campaign of American-style publicity on both sides, said in his victory speech: "Now you can sleep quietly for the next six years." Indeed, once we have seen our representative off to the seats of power, we may as well sleep away the years till our next chance to act.

The cause of democracy's extinction is that political units are so large. A club of twenty members may reach a decision communally; but for a modern city, let alone a nation, this is not practical. So one way of bringing allocracy nearer to democracy would be to reduce the size of political units. The world might be broken down into hamlets and bands as in the far past; or the large units which we have might be subdivided. In the system of "basic democracies" set up by former President Ayub of Pakistan, representatives to councils were elected by groups of only about a thousand voters, and thus must have been really well known to them and perhaps influenced by them. Yet this was still basic allocracy, not basic democracy. The representatives were themselves represented at a higher level by fewer representatives, who were thus at a further remove from the people. It is hard enough for us to influence a first screen of representatives, without having to depend on them to do even our influencing for us at the next level.

The only power of the people, in a representative system, is the dilute and dubious power of influence. We can hope to influence our representative in several ways:

We can decide to vote against him next time; we can murder him, rebel against him, impeach him, bribe him, criticize him or stir up discussion about him; we can grumble unconvincingly in the newspapers that we didn't intend our vote as a mandate for this but only for that; or we can write letters to him. This last seems the weakest of all but I pick it out as hopeful.

Writing a letter to a representative is a direct expression of opinion on a single issue. But it has, on average, almost no effect. If the opinion is contrary to that held by the representative, it is not likely to change his mind and he will ignore it. If it supports him, and he happens to be sponsoring a bill on this point, he will be able to use it as ammunition. But the chances are ninety-nine to one that a letter will not go to the right senator, for instance. Thus ninety-nine percent or so of the great energy expended in writing these letters is wasted, and the evidences of public feeling are filed away in obscurity.

But let's suppose that a governmental institution is set up to which letters may be sent, instead of or as well as to representatives. Representatives (congressmen, the head of state, other officials) would be required to send letters from constituents, or copies of them, to the institution. We could call this institution the Public Opinion Clearinghouse, and the civil servant in charge of it the Public Opinion Monitor. And letters addressed simply to the Public Opinion Monitor, as well as those to legislators,, would find their way to the clearinghouse.

In the clearinghouse, the opinions of the letter-writers would be registered by a classificatory system, perhaps related to the existing statute book. (If the Patent Office can develop a classification for every gadget, then the Public Opinion Clearinghouse can develop one for every facet of government.)

Legislators wishing to speak on some issue would be able to mention the quantity of letters received not just by themselves but by congress and government as a whole. This would be a much more significant figure—less liable to distortion because larger and because not affected by the interests the legislator himself is known to have.

But there may be letters on issues which no legislator is prepared to raise. So let's further suppose that, as soon as the letters urging a certain measure pass a certain number (say, one thousand), the Public

Opinion Monitor is required to organize a referendum, provided that a referendum has not been held on the same point for a certain length of time (say, two years).

A leaflet would be printed, in which both sides would be allotted the same amount of space for setting out their case. The arguments in the leaflet would be written by legislators if there were any who supported them; otherwise volunteers would be sought from among those who had written letters on the subject. The leaflet would be printed by the Public Opinion Clearinghouse, in the same format throughout. It would be a concertina-shaped piece of paper, like many commercial leaflets. The case for change would be printed on one side, the case for non-change on the other. Thus neither side of the paper would be the beginning of the leaflet.

Supplies of this leaflet would then be available in post offices and handed over free to any voter who asked for it and produced proof of identity, upon which the voter's name would be marked on a list as at a polling station. The leaflet would then be returned any time between a day and a week later, with the vote recorded on it in the space provided. This would come as near as possible to ensuring that everyone who voted would have read the cases of both sides presented as fairly as possible.

And in this way a piece of legislation could be carried through entirely without the help, hindrance, or other intervention of politicians. It would be started by citizens, even if no politician had undertaken it; it would grow if a sufficient number of citizens felt a need for it; and it would finally become law if a majority of citizens wished for it, no politician having power to prevent it.

It may seem derisory that such a great result should be initiated by letters of opinion sent to officials. Such letters are now written by few except cranks, compulsive letter-writers, and special-interest groups. But that is because of the general ineffectiveness, or merely random effectiveness, of writing letters when there is no institutionalized function for them. Compare letter-writing with voting. They seem utterly different processes, but the difference lies mainly in what is done with the vote or letter after it has been received. The votes are counted and have a prescribed legal effect; the letters are not (or only desultorily) counted and have no necessary effect at all. So most people vote, but few people write letters to government, whether or not they feel like expressing an opinion. How many would vote if they knew that their votes were going to be regarded as merely advisory expressions of opinion, to be counted and used if and only if an individual recipient felt like counting and using them?

Leaving aside the details, it is clear that such a legislative mechanism would be a truly democratic one. Without meeting together, but also without having to work through intermediary representatives, the people themselves would decide on at least some of the laws they live under.

There are two democratic mechanisms in existence already: the referendum or plebiscite, and the ballot proposition or "initiative." The national referendum, as practised for instance in France, allows the whole people to exercise an absolute decision, but it is not very democratic because it is only occasional and is taken at a moment and on an issue autocratically chosen by the president. The propositions put on ballots in many American states and in Switzerland are more democratic but not completely so. Their content is not decreed by the rulers, but it is decreed by small groups. They are quite frequent, but they still cover only a small fraction of the business of legislation. They apply only to a state, not fhe nation. The heading printed over these propositions in the California ballot paper— "MEASURES SUBMITTED TO VOTE OF VOTERS"—suggests a kind of puzzled discovery: that the voters may actually vote for things, instead of voting for other voters to vote for things for them! To make this system of propositions into a basis for a fuller democracy, we should principally have to find a way to get the propositions initiated, and not merely approved, by the will of the people. Letters provide a way to do this.

So we could, even in a large country, agree to submit ourselves to true democracy. That does not mean we would necessarily like the result. If the majority of the people really determine what is to be done, they may determine things that we as individuals judge to be crass or base. When we think about it, we may well decide that it's safer to go on assuming that a minority of elected officials is wiser than the majority that elected them. All I'm doing is putting to a test our pious admiration for democracy. We say we want it, and I think there is a way we could have it.

My notes tell me that in 1965, when I conceived this plan and discussed it with as many people as I could so as to become aware of objections to it, I heard only two that could not be met by modifications within the plan:

— "It would put power in the hands of an intellectual minority, who alone will write the letters and read the leaflets." (Whereas now people vote without necessarily having read anything; or, more typically, have read or heard polemics on one side but not on the other. In any case one would be able to record a vote on the leaflet without actually reading it; while the letters would only initiate issues, not decide them. Power is at present in the hands of a much smaller intellectual minority: for if "those who are able to write letters and read leaflets" can be called a minority, then "those who are able to make speeches and campaign for office" certainly can.)

— "It would depersonalize the argument, which should be carried on between speakers on television." (I can only flatly disagree that television, and personality, provide a more desirable argument than print, and impersonality.)

There are probably more formidable objections to raise. A pressure-group that can organize such an initiative could do a lot of harm. But so can orators, and ignorance.

A dream at Taroudant

I had been thinking about a dispute going on within Amnesty International. I imagined a vote by direct democracy. That is, my old idea that voting should be on a printed ballot, each candidate or proposal having to state its case in plain prose on one page or panel of the ballot document. But someone objects: "You can make them vote by marking the ballot, but you can't prove that they've read the statements!" I reply: "Yes, you can. It happened in a vote for the board of the Philanthropic Society of West Wensleydale. They required the candidates to submit their statements with double spaces dividing the sentences (the way I write). Then they wrote a little computer program that broke up the statements into sentences and made an array of all those sentences. Then each voter got a ballot and a sentence randomly chosen by the computer; and had to return the vote along with the correct answer as to which statement the sentence came from.

"That hasn't really happened yet, but I could write the program in half an hour and the program would do the job in a fraction of a second, and it would prove that the voter had read the statements, with sixty percent certainty. Make it three random sentences and it would be eighty percent certainty . . ."

It's often hard to tell where dreaming passes into waking; the words may not have been as spoken in the dream, but the essence of them was. This was a dream not only of the type that seems real while being dreamed, but of the smaller type embodying an idea that seems, to the half-waking dreamer, practical, and of the almost vanishingly smaller subtype that still, on waking, seems practical. Therefore it kept me awake for the rest of the night.

www.ingramcontent.com/pod-product-compliance
Lightning Source LLC
Chambersburg PA
CBHW060045040426
42331CB00032B/2469